THE
PERSUASIVE
COPYWRITER

E.N.J. Carter

ISBN: 978-1547095353

Contents

Introduction

I begin this guide reluctantly. I said I might write one when my advertising career was over, but got propelled into teaching. That phase of my life has just ended, so now I'm stuck with either doing this guide, or not doing it. In my career as an advertising copywriter, I was fired a number of times, and stormed out of two other positions. In all cases, I believed, for the sake of my craft.

No one was going to tell me how to create an ad. In my thinking, my bosses had never played Ringalevio (Google it); shimmied up three stories between buildings to sneak into the Bronx Winter Garden to watch wrestling matches; or understood what real people were thinking, not focus groups. I was a street kid from the South Bronx. A curse (telling people exactly what was on your mind) and a blessing (never relying on anyone but yourself).

That said, neither my mother, nor my Irish relatives, ever understood what a copywriter was. In fact, most people today, I'm sure, still think a copywriter is someone who copies things all day, not understanding that copy is from a newspaper term, and that copywriters were creative, not copy cats. Trouble is, I may not know what it means to be a copywriter today. I'm puzzled by phases like 'Content.' What does that exactly mean? When I hear the term, I think of filler: Space occupied by words for their own sake. I only know what I know to achieve what I did and am passing it along for what it's worth. Of course, I do have an opinion about the advertising business today.

The business of Advertising, as I see it, is now broken into two parts: traditional and the Internet More specifically, I think of traditional as being persuasive, and the Internet as being based on behavior.

Is there such a thing as a 'behavior' concept? I don't think so. To be blunt, I believe a lot of brands are wasting their money on the Internet. No persuasion, just: 'like my brand' through innuendo suggested in social media, or a banner ad, or an intrusive video. And anyone who calls themselves a copywriter for just supplying 'content' is fooling themselves. Worse, I've seen portfolios with no headlines and no body copy turned out by students enrolled in expensive portfolio programs. Give me a break. They're not learning anything about being persuasive. At best, they think a visual pun is going to convince a consumer to buy the product they're advertising. The ads scream for 'brandness,' but there is none: just visual puns that force every brand into the same category: nice to look at but no 'sell.' Basically, all the ads look the same, because the thinking for each ad is the same. No thinking.

Unfortunately for those advertisers wasting their money on the Internet, there is no 'model' yet for digital as there is for traditional: the 30-second TV commercial. I suspect videos with a strong narrative drive will take hold to some degree. But I'm full of prejudice against digital approaches, and think agencies that call themselves digital are snake-oil salesmen.

For what it's worth, I first became interested in advertising when I used to sit in front of the radio (Welfare families in my time were not allowed to own TV sets) and eagerly consumed Quaker Oats when the Quaker Oats commercial came on during "Sgt. Preston of the Yukon".

Radio jingles like "Lucky Strike Means Fine Tobacco" probably had a great deal of influence on me, as well.

And certainly, while it may seem odd, the only thing I remember from high school was when the substitute English teacher said his friend had written *Ronzoni Sono Buono*. Wow, for some reason that seemed a lot more interesting than learning about past participles.

Advertising seemed so logical to me; a channel for creativity without needing a brush in your hand, or an MFA in writing. Anyone could do it if they were smart enough. But advertising is a business, and business has no conscience. "What have you done for me lately?" is an understatement. "Creatives" are perceived as the feminine side of the business. The perception in the past was always that it's the account guy, or new business woman who goes out and gets the business, or keeps the business. And then there's the ego-shattering problem of someone always trying to take credit for your work. Most left-side of the brain thinkers can't help themselves when it comes to trying to take credit for someone else's idea.

And you also might consider: Is it normal for a human being to even give a crap about creating the best tuna-fish ad ever done? What drives a copywriter to want to create a jingle, or convince someone to eat their client's chicken, and not a competitor's?

While there are many college programs for art directors, there are few for advertising copywriters, who are the other half of an advertising team. And the truth be known, most copywriters want to become screen writers, and there's always an unfinished script somewhere in their office. But once advertising becomes a means to an end, that copywriter usually burns out, and eventually becomes known in the business as a hack. Lots of hacks fill commuter trains. It's where they devise their best scheming to survive, and keep their jobs so their kids can stay in college. You see, oddly, great advertising demands passion, even for a can of tuna fish. It's the least we can do for our clients. And when the passion runs out, the scheming begins. You witness the results of that scheming every night when your view those terrible ads on television that waste the client's money.

In my case, little did I know that typing specifications and charges for summary, special court-martials, as well as undesirable discharge boards, and article 32 investigations for general court-martials, as a PFC in a Combat Maneuver Battalion on the East German border, would give me the confidence to want to pursue the goal of being an advertising copywriter. At the time, however, there were few opportunities for future copywriters with a street-kid background.

In my advertising career, I would end up in Miles Davis's bedroom (not what you think), make a creative new business pitch in Kuala Lumpur while someone played cocktail piano, spend eighteen days on the highways of Australia, commute back and forth to Singapore, almost get stabbed by a Bedouin in Sinai, get fired in London, and write Janis Joplin's obituary ad. These are just a few of examples of how varied the life of a copywriter can be.

This book is a culmination of my thirty-plus years as a copywriter and eleven years teaching copywriting at Pratt, Syracuse University, and School of Visual Arts. I'll have more to say about my take on the teaching of advertising, but that's later on in this guide.

So the brief for you is to finish reading this book; you might learn something.

Fantasy vs. Imagination

Constantin Stanislavski, the famed Russian director, wrote, "Imagination creates things that can be or can happen, fantasy invents things that are not in existence, which never have been or will be."

It's the fantasy part, in my opinion, that is the downfall of so many Super Bowl commercials. How can we believe something that is not true? 'Wait a minute,' you're saying. 'I went to see a movie about gangs in space and believed every minute of it.' Well, I might add, this is because you knew when you paid the admission fee you were willing to suspend your disbelief on this latest scientific thriller.

You haven't paid to suspend your disbelief when looking at an ad.

Truthfully, as consumers, we don't like something shoved in our face. We haven't paid for the privilege. While fantasy can be entertaining, it's wrapped up in make-believe. It doesn't hit us emotionally if it's a company trying to sell us a product. There's no truth to the premise. It may entertain us, but not motivate us. It doesn't seem *real*.

In a basic advertising course I taught for eleven years at School of Visual Arts, I used to give what I called a "Communicate Piece" to students who had never done an ad.

The brief was to do a poster on why dog owners should not allow their dogs to pee on trees; that dog urine suffocated tree roots.

Inevitably, I would get a few ads with the tree talking to the dog owner. Basically, fantasy that a dog owner might find amusing, but not convincing.

However, I believe, at the heart of every effective communication is truth. How true can your ad be to the consumer? Truth penetrates, and can be conveyed in an imaginative way (For example, a sign on the tree that points to the nearest fire hydrant and explains that dog urine suffocates roots.)

On the other hand, the curse of fantasy of a tree talking might be helped with a headline that said, "If This Tree Could Talk, This is What It Would Say to You." Or a sign that said, "Look at the jerk who's letting his dog pee on me." Again, try to make the premise as truthful as you can. This is an important consideration when it comes to persuasion.

Basically, the exaggeration should come from the consumer benefit. To paraphrase William Bernbach, the founder of Doyle Dane Bernbach (the genius who put the art director and copywriter together way back in the fifties), "If you're going to show me a man upside down, I hope you're selling me something that prevents coins from coming out of his pockets."

The Anatomy of an Ad

Oy, the times I have seen a major campaign try to be creative at the expense of the product benefit. A product with a difference that is not at the heart of the communication is a tragedy in my opinion. Advertised as if the benefit is the same as that of its competitors. The problem, most, times is not enough thinking has gone into looking to see if the product has a difference. Or how to spot it. Not seeing the forest for the trees, so to speak. The 'benefit' often gets lost, because the ad is not approached as two parts:

1. What do you want to say?
2. How do you say it?

The "What do you want to say?" part is crucial. Before knowing what you want to say, you have to determine:

a) Does the product have a meaningful difference?
b) If no difference what's the best way to maximize the product benefit?
c) Or is the Brand Attribute the best thing I can say about the product?
d) Or am I missing the whole point? A marketing difference is driving the ad.

And don't forget to ask, after wasting an hour talking with an account person about the brief, 'What's the reason for the ad?' As obvious as that sounds, that kind of common sense is not endemic amongst left-side of the brain thinkers.

Another consideration is 'Intrinsic Interest.' Basically, what kind of message would the consumer get if you just showed the product? We know a Number 2 Pencil isn't as intrinsically interesting as a photo of a new BMW. Which is why celebrities are used for products with low intrinsic interest.

This is basically a cop-out in my opinion. However, Michael Jackson was a lot more interesting than a bottle of Pepsi, and did a lot for the Pepsi brand. Sometimes it works.

When we think about it, most of us instinctively know how interesting the product or service we're working on is to the public. The less the interest, we know the harder we'll have to work at getting our message across. So many agencies overdo it, however, with 'borrowed interest.' You know, 'If you hold a man upside down, I hope you're selling me something that prevents coins from coming out of his pockets.'

Complicating matters a bit, is the fact that the only thing that sticks in the public mind may be the brand attribute, which I'll discuss in one of the following chapters.

Searching for a Product Difference

For me, searching for a product difference is like searching for the Holy Grail. I spent my whole career annoying account people and clients for more information about their product. Sometimes it could be embarrassing. Once I made at least sixteen calls to the Maxell Client trying to find out what the difference was between their 'Gold' VH video tape and their lower-priced tape. Yet, I could not find out. Finally, I obtained the telephone number of their Hong Kong plant. The supervisor of the plant wasn't expecting it but I broke through his defenses with specific questions like "Are the tapes made on different machines?"

He confessed they weren't, and stated that the 'difference' between the more expensive Maxell brand, and the cheaper brand was the 'nicks' in the cartridge.

The Gold tape was perfect, so to speak. Talk about embarrassing.

The first thing a copywriter should ask if they do discover a difference in the product or service they're working on is 'does it really mean anything? What's the consumer benefit, if any?'

If the shutter on a Nikon was made of slightly better material than that of their competition, does it matter? Maybe it matters if you think about using it in an "Only Ad." For example, your headline says, "Nikon is the only camera with (list a few features every camera in Nikon's class has), and then add the shutter information which the other cameras don't have. I believe the shutter information by itself would have been boring, but the 'only' aspect leaves a bigger impression, weaselly as the headline is.

One of the best ways to find out about the product you're working on is to go to the competitor's web site. What are they *not* saying that your product's web site *is* saying? I guess you could call it 'deductive logic.'

Some of you reading this are probably saying, "You idiot, all you do is ask the client or product manager." Unfortunately, that's never been enough for me. Simply stated, product and brand managers come in all shapes and sizes, and many don't understand the idea behind competition.

I have worked with clients, hard to believe, who don't want to get in a pissing match with their competition. They think they can control the market place by not saying certain things about their product that may be better than the competition. Castrol Motor Oil was such a client. They had signed an agreement with Quaker State not to make superior claims because of a law suit. Anyway, I won't bore you with the details, but after I created the product claim, "Maximum Protection against Viscosity and Thermal Breakdown," they finally went with it to great success, although it was like pulling teeth to get their chemist to agree to the claim.

Basically, competition scares a lot of clients. And then there's the networks themselves who get a preview of TV storyboards—or once did, anyway—and try to dilute superior claims by products in the same category as their big-spending brands. You wouldn't believe how hard we had to fight to get the Castrol claim on the networks, because Quaker State had a much larger TV network budget.

To sum things up, any copywriter who works on an ad without trying to find out if it's a better product than its competitors, should be forced to write banner ads for the rest of their career.

The No-Product
Difference Approach

Call it what you want. This technique was developed by pioneering agencies in the 1960s—two that stand out are Wells Rich and Greene, and Jack Tinker. I first learned of this technique when I took Bill Casey's Copy Course. Casey was an advertising genius. Helmut Krone, in the biography written by Clive Challis is quoted as saying that everything he knew about advertising was because of Bill Casey, who worked as his copywriter at Doyle Dane Bernbach. Interestingly, it could be argued that Krone's words include credit to Casey for the 'look' of the early Volkswagen ads, and the Polaroid ads often credited to Krone, which made him famous.

I personally heard Casey say, in one of his nighttime copy classes, regarding the initial Polaroid assignment,

"I told Helmut I didn't want to write copy. A photo and one line of copy underneath should do it," or words to that effect.

Unfortunately, in those days, the only Advertising award show in town was run by the Art Director's Club. Writers' names were not included in their yearly award book. So Helmut got all the credit. Casey should be in the Advertising Hall of Fame, but that's another story.

Anyone taking Casey's expensive nighttime course (At the time Casey's day job was being creative director at a major New York Agency) had to be able to do a great ad for a product that was the same as all the other products in its category. A daunting challenge for beginners. The 'great' part meant you had to choose a target statement and 'swing it.' One of the best examples of this type of advertising technique was the campaign for "Oh, the disadvantages of the new Benson & Hedges 100's." The cigarettes at the time were the same length as Pall Mall 100's, but instead of emphasizing the benefits of that length, the campaign highlighted the 'disadvantages' of a longer cigarette. Like getting caught in an elevator door, or burning a hole in the newspaper you were reading, etc.

Notice, the 'negative' of the approach is really the 'positive,' as the negative highlights the 'perceived' consumer benefit (at that time) of a longer cigarette.

Simply stated, the secret is:

The worst thing that can happen when you exaggerate the best thing about the product.

The genius of this approach is your 'exaggeration' is coming from a basis of truth and is not wallpaper out there trying to get the viewer's attention by merely entertaining him or her like so many failed Super Bowl commercials.

You've given the reader or viewer *Permission to Believe*.

The logical way to approach this way of thinking is to pick more than one consumer benefit to begin with, and do an ad for each 'target statement.' A rug, no different from any other rug, for instance, can be comfortable, or beautiful, or durable, etc. Can a rug be so comfortable you fall asleep every time you stretch out on it? You get the idea.

I would like to point out at this time that you are using this technique because you've decided the product you're working on has the same product benefit as others in its category. So your job is to make that benefit really penetrate the reader's mind in a way that the competition has not. The exaggeration must have a Permission to Believe, which always happens if you work with the consumer benefit of the product—your target statement.

Simple, but not so simple. You head should be hurting when you come up with the final ad.

The Brand Attribute

Regarding 'What Do You Want to Say?' you've decided the product doesn't have a real difference regarding the consumer compared to the competition's product. On the other hand, it does have a difference regarding the brand. Ketchup is almost a commodity product. You buy the cheapest brand that's on sale. On the other hand, Heinz has a brand attribute for pouring slow, which translates to more tomatoes in the bottle, although that may be hard to prove. Examples of slow pouring might be: a photo of a device that relieves arm exhaustion. You might call it The Heinz Holder. Or a nice juicy shot of Heinz pouring out of a bottle with the headline, "The New York Minute Just got longer." Maybe a bus shelter that shows a bottle of Heinz that says "Slower Than New York Traffic." One of my favorites was a poster done by a student of mine who wrote: "Holding Up Dinner For More than 130 Years."

We know inherently why it would be wrong to advertise Tiffany on a pizza box, but the internet has brands flying all over the place: 'Touchpoints,' and such. If these sites were magazines, the brand wouldn't be seen dead in them. Conclusion: The loss of 'brandness' is endemic, in my opinion, on the social web.

That said, in my experience, there are two types of product or brand managers—those who work directly with the product and are committed to it, and those who are just passing through, making sure their brand stays in the black no matter what. Even taking money out of the national budget for in-store coupon promotions that reduce the brand to a commodity but keep sales in the black. These latter executives are awful to work with. Their only passion is their careers.

Concept Driven by Marketing

This is a campaign where the marketing is the strongest idea. The idea of a creative concept, held prisoner, so to speak, by the information you're forced to convey. One great example, and I'm told misleading, was the 'Frankfurter and Uncle Frank' campaign for a drug that supposedly lowered the "bad" cholesterol not only from food, but inherited from family history. In other words, food and family were both sources of cholesterol. Doing this type of campaign is like trying to solve a puzzle. You know what you have to say, but it's a mouthful by the time you say it. The main point is, you have to recognize your restrictions and the limitations the marketing is putting on you. In other words, you have little chance of getting in the award books working on this kind of campaign.

Permission to Believe

I first heard the term used by a researcher working on the Castrol Motor Oil account. In retrospect, I suspect, Do-It-Yourselfers would not believe a product claim unless something in the commercial affirmed that the claim was true, which makes perfect sense to me.

Examine the early Volvo Ads written by Ed McCabe, who I consider the greatest copywriter in the history of advertising: At the end of his persuasive print ads for buying a Volvo, more often than not, was "That's why 9 out of every 10 Volvos registered here in the last eleven years are still on the road." Basically, whatever Ed wrote in those ads, the clincher was that marvelous fact. You could not walk away from Ed's print ads without feeling that Volvo was a better car.

Of course, Ed, being the genius that he is, never mentioned how many Volvos were actually sold in the

US at that time. Not a lot of Volvos were on the road compared to cars from Detroit.

A Permission to Believe is extremely important when it comes to concepts that use exaggeration. Take the Talking Stain commercial for Tide to Go (2008 Super Bowl); taking a real situation—the 'problem' so to speak—and exaggerating it. The Permission to Believe is the fact that if you walked into a job interview with a 50-cent-sized stain on your shirt, the person interviewing you would be looking at that stain and wondering what the hell is wrong with you. Of course, we kind of have to think the stain was done at the last moment and there was nothing the interviewee could do about it. That said, the stain 'talking' just adds to the damage, we know, that would interfere with everything he said. Which is what happens in an exaggerated way in the commercial.

The Headline

(All ad examples were created by E.N.J. Carter—Earl Carter in the award books)

God forbid, if you ever see more than one or two token headlines in student portfolios these days. Anyway, I'll give you my take on headlines:

1) HEADLINES THAT INTRODUCE THE VISUAL:

To use this approach successfully, you must be careful not to tell the reader what they are going to see in the headline, and rob the visual of its energy.

For example, it shouldn't be: A Nikon Camera Was One of the Few Things on the Space Shuttle that Didn't have a Backup System (Visual: Astronaut holding Nikon)

But: ONE OF THE FEW THINGS ON THE SPACE SHUTTLE THAT DIDN'T HAVE A BACKUP SYSTEM (visual of Nikon camera)

It should not be: Nikon Stands behind its dealers (Visual: Camera dealers standing outside their store with the name of their store prominently displayed.

It should be: NIKON ISN'T THE ONLY NAME WE STAND BEHIND (Same visual, but now store owners' names are being introduced for first time in the visual).

It shouldn't be: If you plan to drink on New Year's Eve, Hertz recommends that you take a taxi.

It should be: IF YOU PLAN TO DRINK ON NEW YEAR'S EVE, HERTZ WOULD LIKE TO RECOMMEND ANOTHER RENT-A-CAR (visual: Taxi-cab)

2) HEADLINE AND VISUAL THAT NEED EACH OTHER TO CONVEY SINGLE MESSAGE (VISUAL/VERBAL 'TENSION')

I first ran across this method in a night class at SVA given by a Doyle Dane Bernbach art director. Oddly, instead of giving an entire class on its importance, he mentioned it in passing, using one of his ads as an example. Like Bill Casey's insights into creating no-product difference advertising, it floored me. It penetrated my brain, made an incredible impression, freed me to be my powerful best at getting a consumer's attention

This technique has won more awards—at least in the past—for creatives than any other, but it's not so easy to master. If you say in a headline 'Test Drive a Volvo' that's pretty boring. But if the visual is a snow-storm, the ad becomes compelling; the visual, in essence, 'fights' the headline.

And one further tip: If the headline is 'straight,' the visual should be provocative. And vice versa. You probably know that already.

In trying to master this approach, it's probably best to think of the visual and verbal saying one thing, needing each other to execute your concept.

One of the first times I used this technique was decades ago when I was a copywriter for CBS Records (Columbia). It was an ad for Miles Davis. It said: BEFORE MILES THIS IS WHAT A BLACK MUSICIAN HAD TO DO TO SELL RECORDS (The visual was a coffin).

3) TAKING ADVANTAGE OF TIMELY EVENTS:

When the stock market crashed, I was on the Volvo account: Since the brand attribute of Volvo was that you might be safer in a crash with a Volvo than any other car in its class, the art director and I took advantage of this unfortunate Wall Street event.

The ad we created ran full-page in the *Wall Street Journal* shortly after the crash: BECAUSE ALL CRASHES ARE UNEXPECTED (The visual was a Volvo parked near the Wall Street subway station).

Another example is the Hertz drunk-driving ad mentioned above.

4) GIVING AN OLD TIRED PHRASE *A NEW MEANING* WITH THE VISUAL:

There are lots of pat phrases we use every day. One, for example, is 'God's Country.'

When I was lucky enough to get the opportunity to create ads for the Israel Government Tourist Office, one of my first headlines was, you guessed it: GOD'S COUNTRY. The visual were photographs of Israel's sky, land, and sea, but of course the 'God part' became a lot more relevant as the client was Israel.

Conclusion: As long as the visual is unexpected, I believe it's okay to use a pat phrase, however, you have to use the phrase as it is, and not change it even slightly. It doesn't work for me if you do that.

5) PLAY ON WORDS:

You have to be very careful with this approach, making sure you are not just using the 'play' to be entertaining, and to get attention. And often the 'play' drives the ad, making the visual almost useless, at best 'supporting' the headline.

I once used a 'play' on words for Grey Poupon, but the 'play' implied a product difference: A LOT OF MUSTARDS HAVE BECOME HISTORY SINCE GREY POUPON WAS INTRODUCED IN 1777.

The Theme Line

As many copywriters have discovered, trying to sum up the essence of a brand or a new creative campaign in five words or less can hurt the brain.

In an essay, which is still on the Internet somewhere, titled: "The Theme Line: The Spearhead of Branding," I wrote, "It is the one element of an ad that separates a great brand from a wannabe brand. Accounts may live or die in the marketplace because of it. What's more, if the stars align properly your great grandchildren may see or hear it."

The opportunity to create a theme line is the greatest assignment that you can have as a creative person. The trouble is, if the account changes agencies, the new agency always tries to change the line—even if it is popular. Blame it on human nature I suppose. Strangely, on the other hand, when an agency does have the creative freedom in a new business pitch to change a theme line they usually wait until the eleventh hour to work on it—Sticking it on the end of their new business creative. It really then becomes a *tag line* . . . a bunch of general words that do not express the essence of the creative in a great way.

Oddly, in some way, the reason why creating theme lines has become such a chore is the lack of respect for the process to begin with.

One example are planners and account people (left side of the brain thinkers) who often like to reduce the theme line to a science. It's why so many theme lines sound like marketing statements. And why so many theme lines that tested well in focus groups fail in the marketplace by nobody ever remembering them.

I don't have a clue what the modern workload regarding day-to-day assignments (How much traditional? How much digital?) breaks down for the average copywriter, but I do suspect there may be the feeling that the incentive for coming up with a great theme line may not be that great. After all, who knows the name of an art director or copywriter who's created a great theme line?

For what it's worth, a great theme line doesn't come out of science, it comes out of a healthy ego. For me, it's the heavyweight championship. All sorts of variables enter the picture to achieve a great line, but none are more important than the confidence to know it can be done.

The ability to recognize a great theme line when it's

just a few words on your computer (in my day, tracing paper) is a rare gift indeed.

I recommend the following if you're lucky enough to have such an assignment: Jot down lines throughout the assignment, a few every day, and then forget about the lines until the end of the week. At the end of the week, start improving the lines. Chances are, a fresh line will pop into your consciousness as you do this. It's when you feel you have total control over the work that the best lines will pop up. Writing down a few lines every day (and not looking at them) gives you 'control'; makes you feel 'safe' until your muse delivers the really good stuff.

On Being Competitive

It's hard to feel sorry for Microsoft but those ads for Apple, "I'm A PC" "I'm A Mac" spots some years ago had me saying "For god's sake, Microsoft Agency, fight back." But alas it was not meant to be. The agency Microsoft used didn't know how to fight back, and ran expensive brand campaigns that made no sense or tried to be "cool," which all of Bill Gates's money could never accomplish. Apple owned "cool." Microsoft owned "big bully or words to that effect."

The Apple agency beat their brains out. There was humor of course, but the overriding message was Apple is cool, Microsoft is not. There isn't a student I had in my advertising class that didn't remember those commercials growing up. Not one could name a Microsoft commercial. There's no doubt in my mind that Microsoft could have held their own competition-wise but just didn't know how. But for god's sake, if you're locked in as the big guy on the block, don't waste your money trying to be cool.

In my day, I often ran into clients who were afraid to be competitive. They felt if they bragged too much about some difference they had, the other guy would develop that feature also. Or they would be sued, or spend a lot of money backing up their claim, so Status Quo was the brief. How ridiculous is that? Your ads should rip the guts out of the competition if you can. Show how your product edge is significant and the other guy's product isn't. After all, it's your job to fight for the client. Don't assume there is no difference. Sometimes what the competitor isn't saying on their website can be a clue. Believe me, the account person isn't going to walk into your office and tell you the reason you're doing the ad is because the client wants to say they're better. For me, the ultimate goal is the client seeing the ad for the first time and saying, "Is that really us? Can we say that?"

Currently, the GEICO ads drive me up the wall. I believe I could destroy them with a campaign that tries to find all the drivers in America who actually got a full fifteen percent off, with search parties searching in the most unlikely places. Their line is always "up to 15% off." A weasel if I ever heard one. Boy, would they stop being funny. Maybe the opening for my campaign might be a full-page newspaper ad that said, "Do you think a company that spends half a billion dollars on advertising is going to give you 15% off?" The fun commercials would follow: search parties in the strangest of places, maybe like floating down the Amazon. You get the idea. Oh, you're saying, what if they can prove they gave 15% off—sometimes. I would use that figure against all the subscribers who didn't get 15% off. It wouldn't be pretty.

PICK EITHER KRISPY KREME OR DUNKIN DONUTS AND TRY TO WRITE A PIECE OF COMPETITIVE BODY COPY. INCLUDE THE NAME OF THE COMPETITOR IN YOUR COPY. GIVE YOURSELF 25 MINUTES.

KRISPY KREME	DUNKIN DONUTS
Founded 1937	Founded 1950
30 kinds of doughnuts	More of a selection – 52 kinds
430 locations	5500 locations
Doughnuts made on site and HOT	Doughnuts delivered in morning – can get stale by afternoon
You can watch doughnuts being made on site	Stores often Boxy – small
Big stores, spotless bathrooms	Customers really like the coffee
Coffee considered not as good as DD	Really a coffee shop that serves doughnuts (only 20% of sales) but also sell more bagels than anyone else.
They serve a 'Sweet beyond Imagination' doughnut. Many Northerners consider them too sweet.	Customers have strong affection for Dunkin Donuts since they were kids.
Pre-packaged doughnuts in supermarkets have hurt the brand	

| Some customers are often 'disappointed' when they get their first taste of a KK. They expected more because of the 'buzz.' | |

Do a competitive ad like this every day. Use the Internet to get the information.

Body Copy (1)

I've often heard agency people who can't write body copy say, "No one reads body copy anymore." I never really respected their opinion so it didn't bother me. But I do believe that if you're a copywriter who can't write body copy, you're an embarrassment to your profession.

On the other hand, I taught copy for eleven years at various times for SVA, Pratt, and Syracuse University. My goal was always to try to get the student to create an ad where you didn't have to read the body copy—the whole essence being in the visual/verbal, And the ad really being a billboard. That said, that's not easily achieved, and there will always be a number of products that need body copy to say why they're better than the other guy.

When students used to show me an ad with a headline that I didn't understand, they would enviably say,

"The body copy will explain the reason for the head-line."

I used to counter that body copy is not for explaining the headline, but for a reader who WANTS TO read your ad for more information after being impressed with the headline and visual idea.

A good rule I believe is always continue your body copy with the same idea as the headline. Common sense, I know, but often not done.

TIP: Try to write a sentence without using a comma. You'll eventually have to, but this forces you to come up with a fresher idea for your next sentence. No comma crutch to lean on.

Body Copy (2)

For a good part of my career I worked for an agency that stated it had no rules, but if you created an ad that wasn't 'clear,' it never made it past the Creative Director's door. So I guess that was a rule, and a big one. The whole idea was to first make the ad clear, and then try to knock it out of the park.

Unfortunately, during the Mad-Man days, there were many agencies that created ads that had the reader saying to themselves, "When I think about it, I get it. I think I know what the advertiser means." I used to think of it as obtuse logic. One well-known agency was particular good at it. I still don't understand what Charlie Chaplin had to do with introducing IBM's first personal computer.

Striving for clarity is not easy. The overall strategy is to make your 'argument' sound factual, even when you don't have that many facts

1. **Use Specific Detail**: It isn't, 'Only the Nikon Z-5 has the X-100 flash feature.' But, 'Only the Nikon Z-5 has the X-100 flash feature which allows you to take flash pictures with no hands.'

2. **Create an example**: 'If you lived in New York and decided to drive to Las Vegas, with the new Honda, your first fill-up would be in Chicago.'

3. **Use Contrast:** Contrast also gives a 'factual feel,' or what might be called, 'Direct opposites.' For example, you can watch Krispy Kreme donuts being made right at the point of purchase, while Dunkin Donuts are delivered once a day by truck.

4. **Comparison:** (in terms familiar to the reader). "Downy Wrinkle Releasing Spray is like a wet iron."

What's the Problem?

It seems to me that an ad that solves a problem is inherently more interesting than an ad that doesn't. Even fresher is as ad that tells us we have a problem we never thought about. For example, an ad introducing windshield wipers for the back of the car: "Volvo discovers it rains in back of the car as well."

Or an ad I created for Nikon lenses that said the really right way to buy a lens was to close your eyes. And went on to describe the 'feel' of a great lens, regarding the focusing ring and such.

I suppose the mother lode of such an ad was the first ad for bad breath with a name coined from Latin that was frightening: Halitosis.

Of course, Problem/Solution has been around a long time, but in thinking about it, it's a driving force in more ads than you might think. Problem/Solution is there even if it doesn't hit you over the head. Take

David Ogilvy's classic headline: "At 60 Miles an hour the loudest noise in this new Rolls Royce comes from the electric clock."

The ad I would suggest is not just about the Rolls Royce being quiet, but about superior engineering solving any problems you might have on the road.

There seems to be a visual trend toward Problem/Solution which wins awards, but I'm not convinced is very persuasive. Example: The Weight Watchers ad which shows a wide door for entrance, and a narrow door for exit.

These ads for me, which look good, deny brand-ness, and are simplistic. The major selling point is exaggerated visually, as if Weight Watchers was no different from other brands that help you lose weight. Yes, I know they help me lose weight, but so do a zillion other programs. Do I believe that Weight Watchers might be more successful at it? Yes, but . . .

Narrative Drive

If you've read up to here, I'm going to give you a gift: something that took me twenty years to learn as an author: "The protagonist (main character) has a problem it gets worse." That's it. Next time you read a thriller or see a movie, analyze the story from that perspective. Obviously, it's not hard to see that a problem getting worse will move the story along, which is the main purpose of narrative: "A connected succession of happenings," I read once.

A good TV spot, in my opinion, must feel like it's *going somewhere* and leads to a 'reveal.' Of course every frame of the commercial must lead up to the 'reveal'. One of my examples: Anncr: Vo: "If You Plan to Drink This New Year's Eve, Hertz would like to recommend another rent-a-car." The reveal is a taxicab. Get it?

It's not hard to figure out that a storyteller who

adds extraneous stuff to his story that has nothing to do with the ending wouldn't be invited back to the camp fire.

Advertisers struggle to reach young viewers on the Internet (they're never told that most young people on the Internet have a program to block ads).

"Selling by innuendo," I call it, and obviously don't approve, but then I don't have a smart phone, either.

In my opinion, copywriters need to know how to write a 'story,' which has been the main source of entertainment ever since humans sat around campfires. I was somewhat astonished in my classes on copywriting, that some students didn't understand that a story had to have a beginning, middle, and ending.

TIP: When you're handed the brief by the account person, or creative director, or whomever, be sure and get them to give you a verbal version of the brief. If they mention something that doesn't sound right, respond right away. Or if you get an idea right away, try to bend the brief to your way of thinking. Get them to sign on to at least explore your thinking. The first moments after getting the brief are the best time.

Deductive Logic

One of the best ads I ever came up with involved deductive logic. It was my first assignment for Scali, McCabe, Sloves, then a legendary agency—if you worked there, you practically didn't have to show your portfolio if you went for another job (at least my experience). Ed McCabe, arguably the greatest copywriter in the history of advertising, was the creative director. Unfortunately, this first assignment had a catch: the executive from Nikon assigned to Houston Space Center couldn't find out if the Nikon camera was going to be on board the space shuttle. The art director and I struggled to come up with an ad that probably would have been approved at most agencies, but not at Scali. Ed hated the ad, and said to me, "How long have you been working on this?" (He never looked at the art director if he thought the ad was bad.)

I decided that the ad would only work if Nikon

was on board the space shuttle. However, getting Nikon's man at the Houston Space Center to cooperate with any information was a struggle. Finally, one Sunday I called him from our office and said, "Level with me, is it going to be on board or isn't it?"

His answer revealed something I hadn't considered: He said the astronauts didn't like the idea of using a professional camera they knew nothing about. They preferred the Hasselblad, which they were familiar with. So I said,

"When will they use the Nikon?"

He said, sheepishly, "Maybe on the fifth launch when they're trained on how to use it."

I then realized that he was mixing up "using the Nikon" with it just being on board, which is why we couldn't get a straight answer out of him.

"Is it going to be on board whether the astronauts use it or not?" I asked, almost accusatorily.

"They'll probably have one F-3 on board, stuck under one of the panels with Velcro," he said, sounding ashamed that it wasn't going to be used on the first flight.

And therein lies the answer that got me two One Show Gold Medals for print and a poster. And one silver for the TV spot.

The next words out of my mouth to the art director were, "One of the few things on board the Space Shuttle that didn't have a backup system" (the space shuttle had four backup systems, which was well publicized at the time).

I later removed "on board". Of course the ad was very believable, because of Nikon's durability reputation. It would have been less so with a Canon.

Because of the ad, the F-3 was used on the next flight, I'm proud to say.

This next example is going to sound hard to believe, but a good example of a client not realizing their potential for a great product claim. Our agency was asked to compete with other agencies for the MCI account. Some background: Due to federal law suits, MCI was responsible for breaking up the Bell Telephone System (local service) which was once controlled by AT&T, now regulated to providing long-distance service only.

MCI was also a supplier of long-distance service only, but had a small share of the market and wanted more of the business market. In discussions with their executives at the time (they mostly talked about the government keeping them from being swallowed up by AT&T).

Some further explanation: By the time we got the assignment, a number of local telephone companies had sprung up due to the breakup of the 'Baby Bells.' Some companies might have two or three companies handling their telephone service (one being a low-rate service but not as dependable as a Baby Bell), and almost always, AT&T handled long distance.

None of us at the agency were informed about businesses having more than one telephone service, as obvious as that may seem now.

Well, it occurred to me that MCI kept emphasizing the business they didn't have compared to AT&T (around ninety-three percent at the time) which was understandable, but they were small potatoes compared to giant AT&T, and everyone knew it.

Well, when you're in a situation like this, there's only one thing to do: go after the big guy.

To be frank, I was not a major player on the new business pitch. I was working on another campaign, Ed had left the agency, and the writers that ED hired were no longer high profile with Sam Scali. Sam put his eggs in another basket, so to speak. However, I was given the print part of the new business pitch.

Here's the deductive logic part: I realized that since MCI only did long distance whenever they were part of the telephone service, they were the dominating long distance company. AT&T might also be used if the lines got too jammed, but was on standby when MCI (lower rates) was part of the company's long-distance telephone service.

When I presented the product claim that whenever AT&T and MCI were part of a company's telephone system, MCI was the dominant phone company, The strategy guy at SCALI said that it was impossible that MCI could be the dominant long-distance company. He kept thinking like the client: the share of the market that the client didn't have.

The client couldn't believe the claim either, but finally, two weeks later, called the agency and said it was true. Too late, the campaign had already been determined; the TV spots done by another team had nothing to do with my claim. Sam asked us to jam the claim into the TV spots but it didn't work, as the spots had nothing to do with the claim. Of course we didn't get the business.

Body Copy (3)

There are probably better examples of the copy that I've taken from a Perdue Chicken ad, but I think this ad does the job of how to be persuasive.

HEADLINE

My chickens eat better than you do.

PROBLEM LEAD

The problem with you is you're allowed to eat whatever you want.

TRANSITION

My Perdue chickens don't have the same freedom. They eat what I give them. And I only give them the best.

MAJOR IDEA

Their diet consists of pure yellow corn, soybean meal, marigold petals—you'd call it health food. My chickens drink nothing but fresh water from deep wells.

BENEFITS

The reason I'm so finicky about what goes into my chickens is simple: a chicken is what it eats. And because they eat so well, Perdue chickens are always tender, juicy, and delicious.

ADDITIONAL PRODUCT FACTS IF ANY

And have a health glow that separates them from the rest.

ASK FOR ACTION

So if you want to eat as good as my chickens, take a tip from me. Eat my chickens.

Follow this format and your copy will have a good chance of being persuasive.

Radio

The mistake of many radio commercials is they try to reach a mass audience. Many copywriters don't understand that radio is one on one. In other words personal. The driver during drive time. The spouse at home, etc. The words used must feel 'close' as if they are directed to one person only.

Unless it's a jingle, I believe thirty seconds is not enough for a radio spot. The listener needs more time to grasp the message. They can't go over it again like a print ad. At one time, sixty seconds was average, but some smart media person figured out a while back that there were a lot of TV spots that were some copy and a jingle, so why not just run the jingle as a thirty-second radio spot. And unfortunately thirty seconds became the standard.

THE EARL CARTER TEMPORARY METHOD
(Until you have your own)
TO MAXIMIZE YOUR CREATIVE UNCONCIOUS.

Materials: Ream of recycled paper (500 sheets); Sharpie (black), tape.

1st Day:

Study assignment, do research, then write the first thing that comes to mind on paper, turn it over, AND DO NOT LOOK AT IT AGAIN.

Keep doing this for **25 minutes** trying to accumulate as many thoughts as you can. But remember only one thought, or visual idea, on each sheet of paper, which you will not look at after you put it down.

If you can't think of anything, write a fact about the product or service you are doing.

If you have a headline, but no visual, just write the headline down, and draw a square or rectangular box for the visual to come. Your creative unconscious will eventually fill in the box with a visual.

2nd Day
Same as first day (25 minutes).

3rd Day
Same as first day (25 minutes).

4th Day
Spend 10 minutes doing same thing as 1st, 2nd, and 3rd day, then put all your thoughts, visuals, and ideas on the wall. At this point, when you look at your work other ideas may suddenly come to mind.

Be sure and put those down too.

5th Day
Finally, with all your work in front of you, narrow your thoughts and ideas down to what you think best answers the advertising brief.

6th Day
Have fun executing the idea you like best; do as many versions of your idea as you can. Remember, an ad is two parts: What Do You Want To Say? Then: How Do You Say It?

TV

Junior copywriters and art directors (or whatever they're called today) often make the mistake of creating a storyboard that has more going on than the viewer can see. To shoot it the way they see it is to have a two-minute commercial. It's the quickest way to have a storyboard killed by the Creative Director who will think the 'Junior' label is well deserved.

In short, the viewer only knows what they see on the screen. They don't know what the characters were thinking or doing before they see them.

TV is a close-up medium, as far as I'm concerned. Too often an amateur storyboard is full of medium shots or long distance shots.

In my day there used to be a pre-production meeting. You would sit in the conference room of the director's office and discuss the commercial. If the director was a big-shot, they would tell you the way they wanted to shoot your spot—wrong. The client approved your storyboard, not the director. Juniors would sit there and let the directors run all over their storyboard, too afraid to say anything. A big mistake. A meeting with the director is the only time you have control over your commercial. You have to lay down the law. Tell him or her you want it shot the way it is on the storyboard. It's human nature to want to change things, even the agency producer might go along with the suggested changes. But, believe me, you'll get the blame when the Creative Director hits the roof. Sad to say, Creatives are always blamed when there is a screw-up.

TIP: If you still have to write headlines (I hope), get yourself a nice large photo of a sofa. When you do come up with a headline that you love, place it over the sofa. If your headline works with the sofa, it's lousy. You have not come up with anything that makes the product you're working on distinctive.

Are You As Good As You Think?

This section is off-brief, I understand, but I feel it is necessary regarding a look at employment for advertising majors, particularly copywriters.

It seems that schools that offer advertising programs are being judged on how many awards the school gets in these money-making student contests by Graphis, The One Show, Andy, and others. One has to consider how much these shows charge for each entry. The entry fees are enormous. Years ago, in an excellent course I took at the School of Visual Arts, the instructor more often than not, and which wouldn't be politically correct today, referred to the line: 'Funny how fat people have fat dogs.' We had to figure out what he meant. One, however, would have to assume, human nature and greed being what it is, that the more entries a school makes, the more winners they will have—whether deserved or not. It's pathetic, I believe, for an instructor to 'tweak' a student's work so that it has a chance to win in a contest.

To be honest, any school that has professional advertising people on staff, and an administration willing to spend tens of thousands of dollars to enter student contests, is going to look great in the student section of award books. 'Shooting fish in a barrel' seems to be an apt description. After all, how can a graphic design professor teaching advertising in the Midwest compete with an award-winning advertising professional in New York, Florida, or California, when it comes to 'tweaking' student ads to be entered in student contests?

Is the student who wins Gold more qualified than the student from Middle America whose entry was not 'tweaked'? I don't think so Therein lies my distaste for these student contests to begin with. The advertising agencies that hire advertising and graphic design majors based on student awards only are being ripped off in many cases in my opinion.

Of course, it could be argued that the student learning under an award-winning advertising professional will have learned more even if their portfolio has been 'tweaked'. Only time will tell in each individual case, I suspect.

Summing Up

These days, in my not-so-humble opinion, advertisers are being screwed. Particularly advertisers who are not household names. You can give me all the arguments you want why social media, analytics, metrics, and whatever is the way to spend your budget, but I don't believe it. There is no substitute for a persuasive message. The feeling when you look at an ad or billboard, that the product advertised is better than the competition, even if it's not.

As an author, Amazon charged me a $100 to promote my book *Doo-Wop Dreams*. They kept telling me how many sites my book cover appeared on—64,000, if I remember correctly. Great, I sold one book. The book cover wasn't enough. And will never be. Give me the budget for a quarter page in the *New York Times*, with some of the reviews my book received, and that would be great. Only, I can't afford a quarter page in the New York Times book section, but that doesn't mean I should throw my money out the window and think being on someone's web page is the same as a sale.

George Orwell should be turning over in his grave with terms like "Unique Visitor." In days past, if the campaign ran and sales didn't go up, the agency was fired. Name brands can afford to piss their money away, but the small advertiser is caught in a vicious web of technology.

In my estimation, a copywriter is a person who is creative, not a person who tries to figure out how to trick the viewer into clicking on a page. There should be another name for that person.

Anyway, I've given you the best I can with this guide. I hope you get something out of it. You can always email me at enjcarter@mindspring.com if you have any questions.